Jumping Jack

Tess has a new computer game, 'Jumping Jack'. Imagine her surprise when Jumping Jack leaps out of the screen and starts to cause mischief all over the house. Read on to find out why . . .

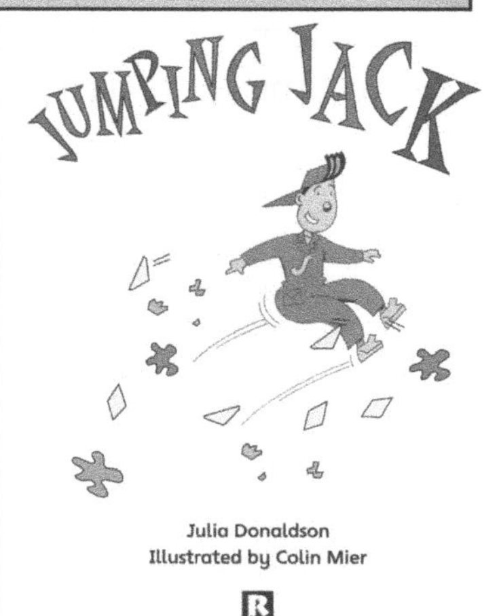

The front cover

Jumping Jack has jumped out of the screen. What sort of character is he?

What do you think might happen in this book?

The back cover

Ask the children to read the blurb.

What problems do you think Jumping Jack could cause around the house?

The title page

What is Jumping Jack doing?

Can the children think of any other words for 'jumping'? (*leaping, springing*)

LESSON 1

Read pages 2 to 5

READ

Purpose: To find out what Jumping Jack's problem was.

Pause at page 5

EXPLORE

What is the problem Jumping Jack has to solve?

Where is Jumping Jack looking for his dog?
(*under the sea, in a valley of dinosaurs*)

Which word on page 5 shows that Jumping Jack has been looking for his dog for some time, and hasn't found him yet? (*still*)

Mum was out. My big brother, Dave, was watching TV. I was playing a computer game called Jumping Jack.

In the game, Jumping Jack was looking for his dog. He was jumping around everywhere. He jumped from hill to hill, then he jumped from reef to reef, but he couldn't find his dog.

Today, Jumping Jack got to another level. He jumped over volcanoes and dinosaurs, but he still couldn't find his dog.

Read page 6

Purpose: To find out what happened to make Jack's mood change.

Pause at page 6

How have Jack's feelings changed? Why is he angry?

Which two words show why the key doesn't fit?
(*rusty, old*)

Read pages 7 to 9

Purpose: To find out what Jack does. Does Tess try to stop him and does he take any notice of her?

Pause at page 9

What does Jack do and where does he go?

Is Tess surprised when Jack jumps out of the screen? How do you know? (*Tess shouted*)

On page 7, what words tell us Jack isn't taking any notice of Tess? (*Jack paid no attention.*) What does 'pay attention' mean?

Find some words to show that Jack is very clumsy. (*knocked over, spilled, made a great mess*)

Jumping Jack went to the next level.
He saw his dog, but the dog was locked
up in a house. Jack had a rusty old key.
He put it in the lock but it didn't fit.
Jumping Jack was so angry that he jumped
up and down all over the screen.

6

Suddenly, he jumped right out of the
screen and on to my desk. He knocked
over a box of disks.
"Hey!" I shouted.
Jumping Jack paid no attention.
He jumped off the desk, down to the
floor, and out of the room.

7

I followed him into the kitchen. Jumping
Jack jumped up on to the table. He knocked
over a pot of jam.
"Stop!" I shouted.

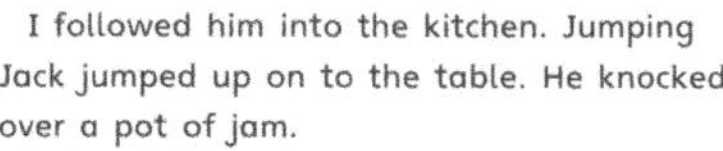

8

Jumping Jack jumped up into
the cupboard. He jumped about and
made a great mess. He spilled the coffee.
He knocked over some cans.

9

READ

Read pages 10 to 13

Purpose: To find out what Jack is looking for. What does he collect?

EXPLORE

Pause at page 13

What has Jack collected so far? Where has he put them? What happens when Tess asks him what he's got?

Who might be cross? (*Mum because of the mess and because of her bath oil, Dave because of his shaving cream.*)

Find the words on page 12 which tell us how Tess tried to get Jack. (*grab him*)

Please turn to page 14 for Revisit and Respond activities.

Then he put a bottle into his sack.
"What's that?" I asked.
Jumping Jack paid no attention.
He jumped back to the table and down
to the floor.

Then he jumped out of the kitchen
and up the stairs. I followed him
into the bathroom.

Jumping Jack jumped into the sink
and out again. I tried to grab him but he
jumped up into the bathroom cabinet.
He spilled Mum's shampoo and knocked
over my brother's shaving cream.

Then he put a bottle into his sack.
"Hey! What are you doing?" I shouted.
But Jumping Jack was off again.

LESSON 2

Recap lesson 1

What were Tess and Dave doing at home?

Why did Jack jump out of the computer?

What has Jack been collecting? Why do you think he's collecting bottles of oil?

How has Jack behaved around the house?

Read pages 14 to 17

Purpose: To find out where Jack goes next.
To find out what happens when Mum comes home and how she reacts to the mess.

Pause at page 17

What does Jack do when he goes back into the computer screen? (*Jack is trying to open the door.*)

How does Tess feel when she hears Mum's car?

How did Mum react to the mess?

Who does Tess blame for the mess?

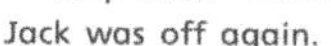

He jumped back down the stairs and
into the workroom. He knocked over the
tool box and spilled some paint. Then
he grabbed a can and put it in his sack.
    "Stop that!" I shouted, but Jumping
Jack was off again.

I followed him back to the computer.
He jumped on to the desk and back
into the screen. Just then I heard a car
drive up. Mum was back!

"What's all this?" she asked when
she saw the mess in the kitchen.
    "Jumping Jack did it!" I said.

"Oh no!" said Mum when she saw
the mess in the bathroom.
    "It was Jumping Jack," I said.

READ

Read page 18

Purpose: To find out how Mum reacts to the mess.

EXPLORE

Pause at page 18

What did Mum say? How do you know she is cross? (*exclamation marks, picture clues, she shouted*)

Who does Tess blame for the mess?

Do you think Mum believes her?

Why did Dave call Mum and Tess?

READ

Read pages 19 to 21

Purpose: To find out what Jack is doing with the bottles of oil.

EXPLORE

Pause at page 21

What does Mum see on the screen that makes her watch more closely?

How do Jack and the dog look on page 20? What's the problem?

Which word is used to show that Jack has tried the key before and it didn't turn then either? (*still*)

What is the last kind of oil that Jack tries, and who does it belong to?

"Look at this mess!" shouted Mum when she looked in the workroom.

"Jumping Jack made the mess, not me!" I said.

Just then my brother called out, "Mum, Tess, look at this!"

He had stopped watching TV and was watching Jumping Jack on the computer instead.

Jumping Jack had just taken something out of his sack. It was a bottle.

"Hey," said Mum. "That's my cooking oil!"

Jumping Jack poured some oil in the lock and tried the rusty key. It didn't turn.

He took another bottle out of his sack. "That's my bath oil!" said Mum.

Jumping Jack tried the bath oil, but the key still didn't turn.

Jumping Jack looked in his sack again. "That's the tool oil!" said Dave.

Read pages 22 to the end

Purpose: To find out if the tool oil works. Does Jack get his dog out?

Pause at page 24

Which oil works on the door?

How can you tell Jack's dog is pleased to be rescued?

Find the words which show that Jack is grateful.
(*thank you*)

Who do you think will tidy up the mess now?

Jumping Jack poured a drop of the
tool oil in the lock. He tried the key
again. This time it turned in the lock.

Jumping Jack opened the door of
the old house. Out ran his dog and
jumped into Jumping Jack's arms!

Then Jumping Jack turned around and
looked at us. He had a big smile on his face.
"Thank you for the oil!" he said.
"Thanks to you I got my dog back."

After Reading
Revisit and Respond

Lesson 1

- Why did Jack jump out of the screen? What was his problem? What problem did Tess have?

- What do you think Mum will say when she gets back? Relate this to the children's experience. What would their mothers say?

- Ask the children in pairs to create a role-play between Tess and Mum. What did Mum say and how did Tess explain what had happened?

- Ask the children to read the story, and list the action words (verbs) which show what Jack did (e.g. *jumped, knocked, spilled, grabbed*).

Lesson 2

- Discuss problems in stories. Explain that having a problem makes a story more interesting. Relate this to other stories the children know, e.g. *The Three Little Pigs* (they had to build a home safe from the wolf).

- Should Jack help clear up the mess? How would he do it? (e.g. *speedily, clumsily – he might make it worse!*) Ask children, in groups, to describe Jack clearing the mess.

- Ask the children which word tells us that Jack is continuing to try to turn the key (*still*). Ask them to brainstorm sentences using 'still', e.g. *I am still doing my homework.*

Follow-up

Independent Group Activity Work

This book is accompanied by two photocopy masters, one with a reading focus, and one with a writing focus, which support the teaching objectives of this book. The photocopy masters can be found in the Planning and Assessment Guide.

PCM F4.1 (*reading*)

PCM F4.2 (*writing*)

You may also like to invite the children to read the text again during their independent reading (either at school or at home).

Writing

Guided writing: Discuss with the group five adjectives that describe Jumping Jack, e.g. *clumsy, careless, quick,* etc. Ask them to write about Jumping Jack using all these adjectives.

Extended writing: Ask the children to write about a time when they needed something (e.g. *a key*), but couldn't find it and had to look everywhere for it.

Assessment Points

Assess that the children have learnt the main teaching points of the book by checking that they can:

- use syntax and context to build their store of vocabulary when reading for meaning (e.g. reading action words, such as 'jumped' and 'knocked').